The Dog and the Bug

Nicole Gueringer

AuthorHouse™
1663 Liberty Drive
Bloomington, IN 47403
www.authorhouse.com
Phone: 833-262-8899

Because of the dynamic nature of the Internet, any web addresses or links contained in this book may have changed since publication and may no longer be valid. The views expressed in this work are solely those of the author and do not necessarily reflect the views of the publisher, and the publisher hereby disclaims any responsibility for them.

Any people depicted in stock imagery provided by Getty Images are models, and such images are being used for illustrative purposes only.
Certain stock imagery © Getty Images.

Illustrated by Yvonne Doane

This book is printed on acid-free paper.

ISBN: 978-1-4634-1399-6 (sc)
ISBN: 979-8-8230-1802-9 (hc)
ISBN: 979-8-8230-1104-4 (e)

Print information available on the last page.

Published by AuthorHouse 11/15/2023

authorHOUSE®

This book is dedicated to all the good in the world.

There once was a bug
who lost his way
and found himself on a sunny day.

Lost in a land he hadn't seen
of fluffy floors and marble beams.

He thought to himself
how could I part
from my loving parents and
their warming hearts.

He circled the floor just to see
fluffy white puppy
starting to proceed

The dog pounced and licked
and started to bark.
The bug shook and shivered
and started to dart.

toward the sun and maybe he'll be.
Back with his family
sipping honey tea.

The puppy pushed and licked
while the bug ran for his life!
Screaming someone please help me!
As he screamed with such fright!

Mrs. Rosey Mother
Mae came into see.
Lifting fluffy puppy and
knelt on her knee's.

Oh Mr. Bug let me help
you some please.

Lifting him up to help him go out.
Back to his loved ones
and bugs all about.

Printed in the United States
by Baker & Taylor Publisher Services